CROCHET

Celtic Crochet Accessories™

By Dot Drake

General Information

Many of the products used in this pattern book can be purchased from local craft, fabric and variety stores, or from the Annie's Attic Needlecraft Catalog *(see Customer Service information on page 15)*.

Contents

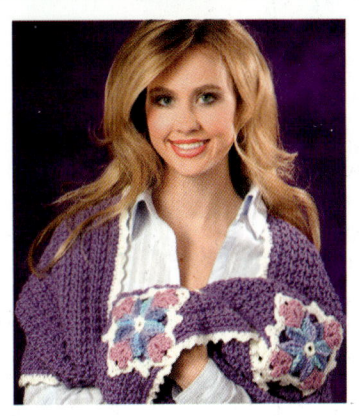

Pocketed Shawl	2
Cloche & Bag	3
Scarf & Hat	5
Footed Lapghan	7
Elegant Evening Wrap	9
Celtic Way Hat & Scarf	10
Little Sister Poncho, Headband & Pouch	12
Big Sister Poncho & Scarf	14
Stitch Guide	16

Annie's Attic • Berne, IN 46711 • www.AnniesAttic.com

Pocketed Shawl

SKILL LEVEL
INTERMEDIATE

FINISHED SIZE
13½ x 66 inches

MATERIALS
- Red Heart Super Saver medium (worsted) weight yarn (8 oz/452 yds/225g per skein):
  - 2 skeins #358 lavender
  - 4 oz/226 yds/113g #311 white
  - 2 oz/113 yds/56g #995 ocean
  - 1 oz/56 yds/28g #530 orchid
- Sizes G/6/4mm and J/10/6mm crochet hooks or size needed to obtain gauge
- Tapestry needle

GAUGE
With J hook: 7 hdc = 2 inches, 6 hdc rows = 2 inches

SPECIAL STITCHES
Beginning double treble crochet cluster (beg cl): Ch 4, yo 3 times, insert hook as indicated, yo, pull lp through, [yo, pull through 2 lps on hook] 3 times, yo 3 times, insert hook in same place, yo, pull lp through, [yo, pull through 2 lps on hook] 3 times, yo, pull through all lps on hook.

Double treble crochet cluster (cl): Yo 3 times, insert hook as indicated, yo, pull lp through, [yo, pull through 2 lps on hook] 3 times, *yo 3 times, insert hook in same place, yo, pull lp through, [yo, pull through 2 lps on hook] 3 times, rep from * once, yo, pull through all lps on hook.

Picot: Ch 3, sl st in top of last sc made.

INSTRUCTIONS
MOTIF
Make 2.

Part A

Rnd 1: With size J hook and white, ch 4, sl st in first ch to form ring, ch 1, 8 sc in ring, join with sl st in beg sc. Fasten off. *(8 sc)*

Rnd 2: Join ocean with sl st in any sc, **beg cl** (see Special Stitches) in same st, [ch 5, **cl** (see Special Stitches) in next st] around, ch 5, join with sl st in top of beg cl. Fasten off.

Part B

With orchid, [ch 5, sl st in first ch to form ring, ch 1, (sc, hdc, dc, ch 1, 3 dc) in ring, ch 3 *(corner ch sp)*, (3 dc, ch 1, dc, hdc, sc) in same ring, ch 8] 4 times, join with sl st in base of first ring. Fasten off.

Place Part B behind Part A, pull corners of Part B through every other ch-5 sp on rnd 2.

Border

Join white with sc in any corner ch-3 sp, (sc, ch 3, 2 sc) in same corner ch-3 sp, *tr in 3rd ch of ch-5 behind corner, ch 1, sc in next ch-1 sp on Part B, (3 sc, **picot**—see Special Stitches, 3 sc) in next ch-5 sp on Part A, sc in next ch-1 sp on Part B, tr in 3rd ch of next ch-5 behind next corner**, (2 sc, ch 3, 2 sc) in corner ch-3 sp, rep from * around, ending last rep at **, join with sl st in beg sc. Fasten off.

Lay Motifs aside.

SHAWL

Row 1: With size J hook and lavender, ch 229, working in **back bar** (see illustration) of chs, sc in 2nd ch from hook and in each ch across, turn. *(228 sc)*

Back Bar of Chain

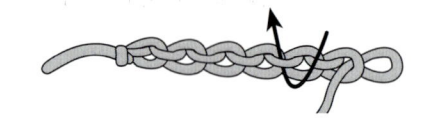

Rows 2–28: Ch 2 (counts as first hdc), hdc in **front lp** (see Stitch Guide) of next st, [hdc in back lp of next st, hdc in front lp of next st] across, turn.

Row 29: With G hook, sl st in each st across. Fasten off.

Pocket
Fold corners of 1 short end tog according to illustration, sew tog. Rep on opposite end.

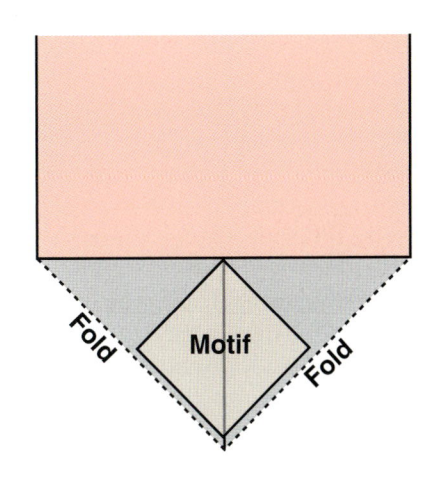

Border
Working around outer edges and across top of Pocket openings, with G hook, join white with sc in any st at one long side, sc in next st, *dc in next sc, ch 2**, sc in each of next 2 sts, rep from * around, ending last rep at **, join with sl st in beg sc. Fasten off.

Sew 1 Motif to each Pocket over seam according to illustration.

Cloche & Bag

SKILL LEVEL
INTERMEDIATE

FINISHED SIZES
Bag: 10 x 12 inches
Cloche: One size fits most

MATERIALS
- Lion Brand Landscapes bulky (chunky) weight yarn (1.75 oz/55 yds/50g per skein):
    2 skeins #540-271 rose garden
- Lion Brands Homespun bulky (chunky) weight yarn (6 oz/185 yds/170g per skein):
    2 skeins #307 antique
- Red Heart TLC Essentials medium (worsted) weight yarn (6 oz/326 yds/170g per skein):
    1 skein #2772 light country rose
- Size I/9/5.5mm crochet hook or size needed to obtain gauge
- Tapestry needle
- Sewing needle
- Blue sewing thread
- 9 pink size 16mm acrylic faceted stones
- 32 blue size 4mm beads
- 2 natural wood 4½ x 6-inch handles
- Tacky glue

GAUGE
With Homespun yarn:
7 sc = 2 inches, 6 sc rows = 2 inches

SPECIAL STITCH
Joining chain space (j-ch sp):

Annie's Attic • Berne, IN 46711 • www.AnniesAttic.com • Celtic Crochet Accessories 3

Ch 1, sc in corresponding ch sp on last Circle, ch 1.

INSTRUCTIONS
CLOCHE
FIRST MOTIF
Circle A
With rose garden, [ch 13, sc in 13th ch from hook] 8 times. Leaving long end, fasten off.

Sew ends tog to form circle.

Circle B
Rnd 1: With antique, ch 4, sl st in first ch to form ring, ch 1, 8 sc in ring, join with sl st in beg sc. *(8 sc)*

Rnd 2: Ch 1, sc in first st, ch 13, [sc in next st, ch 13] around, join. Fasten off.

Secure all ends.

Place Circle B behind Circle A, pull 1 ch-13 of Circle B through ch-13 of Circle A and same ch-13 of A through same ch-13 of B. Rep around with each ch-13, making 8 petals.

Border
Join light country rose with sc in any ch-13 at tip of petal on Circle B, (ch 3, sc) in same ch-13 sp, ch 3, ***sc dec** (see Stitch Guide) in lower part of Circle A of this petal and in lower part of Circle A of next petal, ch 3**, (sc, ch 3, sc) in ch-13 on Circle B at tip of next petal, rep from * around, ending last rep at **, join with sl st in beg sc. Fasten off.

Joined Motif
Circle A
Work same as Circle A of First Motif.

Circle B
Work same as Circle B of First Motif. Secure all ends.

Place Circle B behind Circle A, pull 1 ch-13 of Circle B through ch-13 of Circle A and same ch-13 of A through same ch-13 of B. Rep around with each ch-13, making 8 petals.

Border
Join light country rose with sc in any ch-13 at tip of petal on Circle B, (ch 3, sc) in same ch-13 sp, ch 3, sc dec in lower part of Circle A of this petal and in lower part of Circle A of next petal, ch 3, **(sc, **j-ch sp**—*see Special Stitch* according to illustration, sc) in ch-13 on Circle B at tip of next petal, ch 3, sc dec in lower part of Circle A of this petal and in lower part of Circle A of next petal, ch 3**, rep between ** as many times as needed to join Motifs, *sc dec in lower part of Circle A of this petal and in lower part of Circle A of next petal, ch 3***, (sc, ch 3, sc) in ch-13 on Circle B at tip of next petal, rep from * around, ending last rep at ***, join with sl st in beg sc. Fasten off.

Make and join 3 more Joined Motifs according to illustration.

Glue 1 faceted stone to center of each Motif. Let dry for at least 1 hour.

BAG
PANEL
Row 1: With antique, ch 35, hdc in 3rd ch *(first 2 chs count as first hdc)* from hook and in each ch across, turn. *(34 hdc)*

Row 2: Ch 1 *(does not count as hdc)*, hdc in first st and in each st across, turn.

Next rows: Rep row 2 until Panel measures 20 inches. At end of last row, fasten off.

Fold Panel in half and sew side edges tog.

To attach handles, hdc in each st around, working over handle ends for 3 or 4 sts and making sure handles are evenly spaced, join with sl st in beg hdc. Fasten off.

MOTIF
Make 4.
Work same as First Motif of Cloche.

Glue 1 faceted stone to center of each Motif. Let dry for at least 1 hour.

Position 2 Motifs on 1 side of Bag and sew in place by sewing 1 blue bead to tip of each petal and Bag.

Rep on other side of Bag with rem 2 Motifs. ❑❑

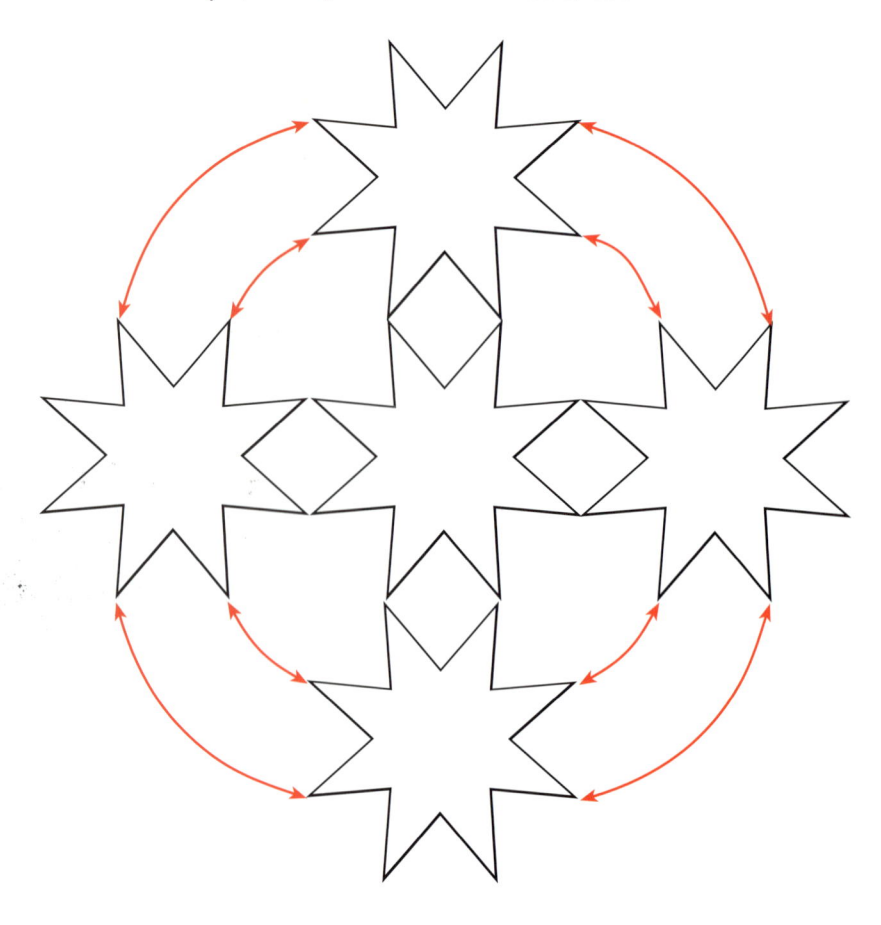

Scarf & Hat

SKILL LEVEL

INTERMEDIATE

FINISHED SIZES
Scarf: 5½ x 54 inches
Hat: One size fits most

MATERIALS
- Red Heart TLC Amore medium (worsted) weight yarn (6 oz/290 yds/170g per skein):
    1 skein #3625 celery
- Lion Brand Landscapes bulky (chunky) weight yarn (1.75 oz/55 yds/50g per skein):
    3 skeins #540-277 country sunset
- Size I/9/5.5mm crochet hook or size needed to obtain gauge
- Tapestry needle

GAUGE
Sc and ch-3 = 1 inch

SPECIAL STITCH
Joining chain space (j-ch sp): Ch 1, sc in Motif to be joined, ch 1

INSTRUCTIONS
SCARF
MOTIF
Part A
Rnd 1: With country sunset, ch 4, 2 dc in 4th ch from hook *(first 3 chs count as first dc)*, (ch 3, 3 dc) in same ch 3 times, join with tr in top of ch-3 forming last ch sp. *(12 dc, 4 ch sps)*

Rnd 2: (Ch 3—*counts as first dc*, 2 dc, ch 3, 3 dc) in ch sp just made, [ch 1, (3 dc, ch 3, 3 dc) in next ch sp] around, ch 1, join with sl st in top of ch-3. Fasten off.

Part B
With celery, ch 5, sl st in first ch to form ring, ch 1, [3 sc in ring, ch 16] 4 times, join with sl st in beg sc. Fasten off. *(4 ch-16 lps)*

Secure all ends. Place Part B behind Part A, matching centers, pull ch-16 lps of Part B to the front through ch-3 sps of rnd 1 on Part A, then pull same ch-16 lps to the back through ch-3 sps of rnd 2 on Part A.

Part C
Rnd 1: Join celery with sc in any ch-16 lp, ch 3, sc in same ch-16 lp for corner, *[ch 3, sc in 2nd dc of 3-dc group on rnd 2 of Part A] twice, ch 3**, (sc, ch 3, sc) in next ch-16 lp for corner, rep from * around, ending last rep at **, join with sl st in beg sc.

Rnd 2: Sl st in corner ch sp, (sc, ch 3, sc) in same corner ch sp, *[ch 3, sc in next ch sp] 3 times, ch 3**, (sc, ch 3, sc) in corner ch sp, rep from * around, ending last rep at **, join. Fasten off.

JOINED MOTIF
Make 10.
Part A
Work same as Part A of Motif.

Part B
Work same as Part B of Motif.

Part C
Rnd 1: Join celery with sc in any ch-16 lp, ch 3, sc in same ch-16 lp for corner, *[ch 3, sc in 2nd dc of 3-dc group on rnd 2 of Part A] twice, ch 3**, (sc, ch 3, sc) in next ch-16 lp for corner, rep from * around, ending last rep at **, join with sl st in beg sc.

Rnd 2: Sl st in corner ch sp, (sc, **j-ch sp**—*see Special Stitch*, sc) in same corner ch sp, [j-ch sp, sc in next ch sp] 3 times, j-ch sp, (sc, j-ch sp, sc) in corner ch sp, *[ch 3, sc in next ch sp] 3 times, ch 3**, (sc, ch 3, sc) in corner ch sp, rep from * around, ending last rep at **, join. Fasten off.

Border

Working around outer edge, down 1 long edge, join country sunset with sc in corner ch sp, ch 3, sc in same ch sp, ◊*[ch 3, sc in next ch sp] 4 times, ch 3, sc in joining, rep from * across to corner, (sc, ch 3, sc) in corner ch sp, [ch 3, sc in next ch sp] across to corner sp◊, (sc, ch 3, sc) in corner ch sp, rep between ◊, ch 3, join. Fasten off.

HAT
MOTIF

Work same as Motif of Scarf.

Joined Motif

Make 3 same as Joined Motif of Scarf.

Last Motif
Part A

Work same as Part A of Motif.

Part B

Work same as Part B of Motif.

Part C

Rnd 1: Join celery with sc in any ch-16 lp ch 3, sc in same ch-16 lp for corner, *[ch 3, sc in 2nd dc of 3-dc group on rnd 2 of Part A] twice, ch 3**, (sc, ch 3, sc) in next ch-16 lp for corner, rep from * around, ending last rep at **, join with sl st in beg sc.

Rnd 2: Sl st in corner ch sp, (sc, j-ch sp, sc) in same corner ch sp, [j-ch sp, sc in next ch sp] 3 times, j-ch sp, (sc, j-ch sp, sc) in corner ch sp, [ch 3, sc in next ch sp] 3 times, ch 3, joining to first Motif to make circle, (sc, j-ch sp, sc) in same corner ch sp, [j-ch sp, sc in next ch sp] 3 times, j-ch sp, (sc, j-ch sp, sc) in corner ch sp, [ch 3, sc in next ch sp] across, ch 3, join. Fasten off.

Brim

Rnd 1: Working around 1 edge of Motifs, join country sunset with sc in any ch sp, sc in same ch sp, 2 sc in each ch sp around with sc in each corner on joined Motifs, join with sl st in beg sc.

Rnd 2: Ch 1, sc in each sc around, join. Fasten off.

Top

Rnd 1: Join celery with sl st in any ch sp on other side of Motifs, ch 3, 2 dc in same ch sp, 3 dc in each ch sp around with dc in each corner sp on joined Motifs, join with sl st in top of ch-3. *(70 dc)*

Rnd 2: Ch 3, [**dc dec** *(see Stitch Guide)* in next 2 sts, dc in each of next 2 sts] around, join. *(47 dc)*

Rnd 3: Ch 3, dc in next st, [dc dec in next 2 sts, dc in next st] around, join. *(32 dc)*

Rnd 4: Ch 2 *(does not count as dc)*, dc in next dc, [dc dec in next 2 sts] around, join with sl st in top of first dc. *(16 dc)*

Rnd 5: Ch 2, dc in next st, [dc dec in next 2 sts] around, join with sl st in top of first dc dec. Leaving long end, fasten off.

Weave long end through top of sts, pull to close. Secure end. ❑❑

Footed Lapghan

SKILL LEVEL
INTERMEDIATE

FINISHED SIZE
56 x 70 inches

MATERIALS
- Red Heart Super Saver medium (worsted) weight yarn (8 oz/452 yds/225g per skein):
    - 5 skeins #995 ocean
    - 2 skeins #358 lavender
    - 2 skeins #311 white
    - 2 skeins #363 pale green
    - 1 skein #530 orchid
- Size I/9/5.5mm crochet hook or size needed to obtain gauge
- Tapestry needle

GAUGE
3 dc = 1 inch, 1 hdc row = ¾ inch

SPECIAL STITCHES
Beginning double treble crochet cluster (beg cl): Ch 4, yo 3 times, insert hook as indicated, yo, pull lp through, [yo, pull through 2 lps on hook] 3 times, yo 3 times, insert hook in same place, yo, pull lp through, [yo, pull through 2 lps on hook] 3 times, yo, pull through all lps on hook.

Double treble crochet cluster (cl): Yo 3 times, insert hook as indicated, yo, pull lp through, [yo, pull through 2 lps on hook] 3 times, *yo 3 times, insert hook in same place, yo, pull lp through, [yo, pull through 2 lps on hook] 3 times, rep from * once, yo, pull through all lps on hook.

Picot: Ch 3, sl st in top of last sc made.

Joining picot (j-picot): Ch 1, sc in corresponding picot of last Motif, ch 1.

Joining chain space (j-ch sp): Ch 1, sc in corresponding ch sp of last Motif, ch 1.

Popcorn (pc): 5 dc in next st, drop lp from hook, insert hook in top of first dc of group, pull dropped lp through, ch 1.

INSTRUCTIONS
MOTIF
Part A
Rnd 1: With white, ch 4, sl st in first ch to form ring, ch 1, 8 sc in ring, join with sl st in beg sc. Fasten off. *(8 sc)*

Rnd 2: Join ocean with sl st in any sc, **beg cl** *(see Special Stitches)* in same st, [ch 5, **cl** *(see Special Stitches)* in next st] around, ch 5, join with sl st in top of beg cl. Fasten off.

Part B
With lavender, [ch 5, sl st in first ch to form ring, ch 1, (sc, hdc, dc, ch 1, 3 dc) in ring, ch 3 *(corner ch sp)*, (3 dc, ch 1, dc, hdc, sc) in same ring, ch 8] 4 times, join with sl st in base of first ring. Fasten off.

Place Part B behind Part A, pull corners of Part B through every other ch-5 sp on rnd 2.

Border
Join white with sc in any corner ch-3 sp, (sc, ch 3, 2 sc) in same corner ch-3 sp, *ch 3, tr in 3rd ch of ch-5 behind corner, ch 1, sc in next ch-1 sp on Part B, (3 sc, **picot**—see Special Stitches, 3 sc) in next ch-5 sp on Part A, sc in next ch-1 sp on Part B, tr in 3rd ch of next ch-5 behind next corner**, (2 sc, ch 3, 2 sc) in corner ch-3 sp, rep from * around, ending last rep at **, join with sl st in beg sc. Fasten off.

Joined Motif
Make 65.
Part A
Work same as Part A of Motif

Part B
Make 23 orchid.
Make 21 pale green.
Make 21 lavender.
Work same as Part B of Motif.

Border
Join white with sc in any corner ch-3 sp, (sc, **j-ch sp**—*see Special Stitches*, 2 sc) in same corner ch-3 sp, j-ch sp, tr in 3rd ch of ch-5 behind corner, ch 1, sc in next ch-1 sp on Part B, (3 sc, **j-picot**—*see Special Stitches*, 3 sc) in next ch-5 sp on part A, sc in next ch-1 sp on Part B, ch 1, tr in 3rd ch of next ch-5 behind next corner, j-ch sp, (2 sc, j-ch sp, 2 sc) in corner ch-3 sp,*tr in 3rd ch of ch-5 behind corner, ch 1, sc in next ch-1 sp on Part B, (3 sc, picot, 3 sc) in next ch-5 sp on Part A, sc in next ch-1 sp on Part B, ch 1, tr in 3rd ch of next ch-5 behind next corner**, (2 sc, ch 3, 2 sc) in corner ch-3 sp, rep from * around, ending last rep at **, join with sl st in beg sc. Fasten off.

Alternating colors, make 2 strips of 13 Motifs each and 4 strips of 10 Motifs each.

BORDER
Rnd 1: Working across 1 short end of 1 Motif strip, join white with sc in corner ch sp, ch 3, sc in same corner ch sp, *ch 3, sc in next ch sp, ch 3, sc in sp between next sc and sc group, ch 3, sc in picot, ch 3, sc in sp between sc group and next sc, ch 3, sc in next ch sp, ch 3, (sc, ch 3, sc) in corner ch sp, [ch 3, sc in next ch sp, ch 3, sc in sp between next sc and sc group, ch 3, sc in picot, ch 3, sc in sp between sc group and next sc, ch 3, sc in next ch sp, ch 3, sc in next j-picot, ch 3, sc in next j-picot] across to last Motif, ch 3, sc in next ch sp, ch 3, sc in sp between next sc and sc group, ch 3, sc in picot, ch 3, sc in sp between sc group and next sc, ch 3, sc in next ch sp, ch 3**, (sc, ch 3, sc) in corner ch sp, rep from * around, ending last rep at **, join with sl st in beg sc. Fasten off.

Row 2: Working in rows across 1 long edge, join ocean with sl st in corner ch sp, ch 3 *(counts as first dc)*, dc in same ch sp, [2 dc in next ch sp, 3 dc in next ch sp] across, ending with 2 dc in corner ch sp, turn. *(174 dc on 10-Motif strip, 227 dc on 13-Motif strip)*

Row 3: Ch 3, dc in each st across, turn.

Row 4: Ch 1, sc in each st across, **do not turn.** Fasten off.

Row 5: Working around post of sts on row 2, with RS facing, join pale green with **fpsc** *(see Stitch Guide)* around post of 2nd dc on row 2, [ch 12, sk next 8 sts on row 2, fpsc around next st] across, **do not turn.** Fasten off.

Row 6: Join lavender with sc in first st of row 4, sc in each of next 3 sts, [ch 1, **pc** *(see Special Stitches)* in center of ch-12 sp of last rnd and in next st on row 4 at same time, sc in each of next 8 sts] across to last ch-12 sp, pc in center of next ch-12 sp and next st, sc in each st across. Fasten off.

Rep rows 2–6 on other long edge of same strip.

Work Border on all rem strips.

Join Strips
With WS tog, matching top edges, sc long edges of 2 strips tog. Fasten off.

Join strips as follows, 2 10-Motif strips, 2 13-Motif strips and 2 10-Motif strips *(the 2 13-Motif strips will be in center with 2 10-Motif strips on each side).*

Bottom Border
Working across bottom edge of 2 10-Motif strips, join lavender with sc in at one corner bottom edge, sc across short panel with 2 or 3 sc in each ch-3 sp. Fasten off.

Rep on bottom edge of rem short panel.

With RS tog, easing to fit, sew extending sides of long panels to ends of each short panel to form pocket as shown in illustration.

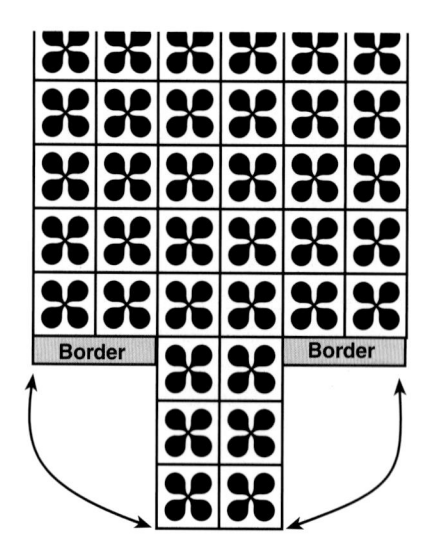

EDGING
Rnd 1: Working around entire outer edge, join lavender with sc in any corner, 2 sc in same st, evenly sp sc around with 3 sc in each corner, join with sl st in beg sc.

Rnd 2: Ch 1, working from left to right, **reverse sc** *(see illustrations)* in each st around with 3 reverse sc in each corner, join. Fasten off. ❑❑

Reverse Single Crochet

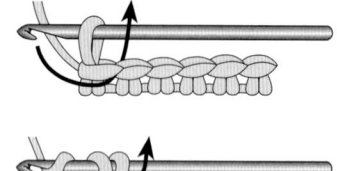

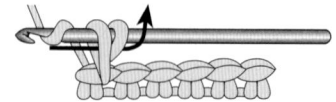

Elegant Evening Wrap

SKILL LEVEL
INTERMEDIATE

FINISHED SIZE
13 x 48 inches

MATERIALS
- Patons Brilliant light worsted (light) weight yarn (1.75 oz/166 yds/50g per skein): 3 skeins each #03005 white twinkle and #03314 lilac luster
- Size I/9/5.5mm crochet hook or size needed to obtain gauge
- Tapestry needle
- Sewing needle
- Sewing thread
- 15 pearl beads

GAUGE
Rnds 1 & 2 = 3½ inches

SPECIAL STITCHES
Beginning double treble crochet cluster (beg cl): Ch 4, yo 3 times, insert hook as indicated, yo, pull lp through, [yo, pull through 2 lps on hook] 3 times, yo 3 times, insert hook in same place, yo, pull lp through, [yo, pull through 2 lps on hook] 3 times, yo, pull through all lps on hook.

Double treble crochet cluster (cl): Yo 3 times, insert hook as indicated, yo, pull lp through, [yo, pull through 2 lps on hook] 3 times, *yo 3 times, insert hook in same place, yo, pull lp through, [yo, pull through 2 lps on hook] 3 times, rep from * once, yo, pull through all lps on hook.

Picot: Ch 3, sl st in top of last sc made.

Joining chain space (j-ch sp): Ch 4, sc in ch-7 sp of specified Motif, ch 4.

INSTRUCTIONS
FIRST MOTIF
Rnd 1: With white twinkle, ch 5, sl st in first ch to form ring, **beg cl** (see Special Stitches) in ring, ch 5, [**cl** (see Special Stitches) in ring, ch 5] 4 times, join with sl st in beg cl. (5 petals)

Rnd 2: Sl st to ch-5 sp, (sc, hdc, 5 dc, hdc, sc) in same ch sp and in each ch sp around, join with sl st in beg sc. Fasten off.

Rnd 3: With lilac luster, ch 13, sl st in 2nd ch from hook and in each ch across, wrap end of ch-13 just made behind petal of rnd 1 to front, join with sl st in beg sl st on ch-13, *ch 5, sc in 3rd dc of next dc group of rnd 2**, ch 18, sl st in 2nd ch from hook and in each of next 12 chs (first 5 chs count as ch-5 sp), wrap end of ch-18 just made behind next petal of rnd 1 to front, join with sl st in first sl st of ch-18, rep from * around, ending last rep at **, ch 5, join with sl st in base of beg ch-13.

Rnd 4: Ch 1, 6 sc in each ch-5 sp around, join with sl st in beg sc. Fasten off.

Rnd 5: Join white twinkle with sc in 2nd sc of any sc group, *ch 4, dc in 4th ch from hook, sk next 2 sc**, sc in next sc, rep from * around, ending last rep at **, join with sl st in beg sc. Fasten off.

Rnd 6: Join lilac luster with sc in any ch-3 sp, *ch 7, sc in next ch-3 sp, ch 7, sc in next ch-3 sp, **picot** (see Special Stitches)**, sc in next ch-3 sp, rep from * around, ending last rep at **, join. Fasten off.

JOINED MOTIF

Rnds 1–5: Work same as rnds 1–5 of First Motif.

Rnd 6: Join lilac luster with sc in any ch 3 sp, [**j-ch sp** (see Special Stitches) in last Motif, sc in next ch-3 sp] twice, picot, sc in next ch-3 sp, *ch 7, sc in next ch-3 sp, ch 7, sc in next ch-3 sp, picot**, sc in next ch-3 sp, rep from * around, ending last rep at **, join. Fasten off.

First Row

Work [Joined Motif joining to last Motif leaving 4 ch-7 sps at bottom unworked between joining; join next Motif leaving 6 unworked ch-7 sps at bottom between joinings] twice, join next Motif leaving 4 ch-7 sps at bottom unworked between joinings, for a total of 7 Motifs in first row.

Second Row

Work Joined Motif, joining to First and 2nd Motifs of First Row; join next Motif to 3rd, 2nd and last Motif, join next Motif to 3rd and last Motif; join next Motif to 4th, 3rd and last Motif, next Motif to 5th, 4th and last Motif, next Motif to 5th and last Motif, next Motif to 6th, 5th and last Motif, last Motif to 7th, 6th and last Motif, for a total of 8 Motifs.

BORDER

Rnd 1: Join lilac luster with sc in 2nd unworked ch-7 sp of last Motif on First Row, *[ch 5, tr in 5th ch from hook] twice, sc in next ch-7 sp, ch 5, tr in 5th ch from hook**, sc in next ch-7 sp, rep from * around always working in 2nd unworked ch sps between Motifs, ending last rep at **, join with sl st in beg sc.

Rnd 2: Sl st to first ch-5 sp, (sc, ch 3, sc, ch 3) in each ch-5 sp around except across bottom edge, across bottom edge (sc, ch 3, sc, ch 3) in each ch-5 sp working (sc, ch 3) in ch-5 sps between Motifs, join. Fasten off. Sew 1 bead to center of each Motif.

Celtic Way Hat & Scarf

SKILL LEVEL
INTERMEDIATE

FINISHED SIZES
Scarf: 7 x 60 inches
Hat: One size fits most

MATERIALS
- Lion Brand Jiffy bulky (chunky) weight yarn (3 oz/135 yds/85g per skein):
  3 skeins #106 baby blue
- Lion Brand Jiffy Thick & Quick super bulky (super chunky) weight yarn (5 oz/84 yds/140g per skein):
  2 skeins #209 Catskills
- Sizes I/9/5.5mm and K/10½/6.5mm crochet hooks or size needed to obtain gauge
- Tapestry needle

GAUGE
Size I hook: 3 dc = 1 inch, 3 dc rnds = 2 inches

INSTRUCTIONS

SCARF
FIRST MOTIF
PART A

Rnd 1: With size I hook and baby blue, ch 4, sl st in first ch to form ring, ch 1, 8 sc in ring, join with sl st in beg sc. *(8 sc)*

10 Celtic Crochet Accessories • Annie's Attic • Berne, IN 46711 • www.AnniesAttic.com

Rnd 2: Ch 8 *(counts as first tr and ch-4)*, [tr in next st, ch 4] 7 times, join with sl st in 4th ch of beg ch-8.

Rnd 3: Sl st to ch sp, (sc, ch 1, 3 dc, ch 1, sc) in same ch sp and in each ch sp around, join with sl st in beg sc. Fasten off.

Part B
With size K hook and Catskills, [ch 12, sl st in 11th ch from hook] 8 times. Leaving long end, fasten off.

Sew ends tog forming a circle, being careful not to twist.

Lay Part A on top of Part B, pull each ch-12 of Part B through each ch-4 sp of Part A from back to front.

Border
Join baby blue with sc in last dc of dc-group, ch 3, *sk sc and ch-1 sps, sc in first dc of next dc-group, ch 3, working in front of ch-12 on Part B, dc in next dc, ch 3**, sc in next dc, ch 3, rep from * around, ending last rep at **, join with sl st in beg sc. Fasten off.

JOINED MOTIF
Make 9.
Part A
Work same as Part A of First Motif.

Part B
Work same as Part B of First Motif.

Border
Join baby blue with sc in last dc of dc-group, ch 3, sk sc and ch-1 sps, sc in first dc of next dc-group, ch 3, working in front of ch-12 on Part B, dc in next dc, [ch 2, sc in corresponding ch sp on last Motif, ch 2, sc in next dc on this Motif] twice, ch 1, sc in next ch sp of last Motif, ch 1, working in front of ch-12 on Part B, dc in next dc, ch 1, sc in next ch sp of last Motif, ch 1, sc in next dc on this Motif, [ch 2, sc in next ch sp of last Motif, ch 2, sc in next dc on this motif] twice, ch 2, sc in next ch sp of last Motif, ch 2, working in front of ch-12 on Part B, dc in next dc on this Motif, ch 3, [sc in next dc, ch 3, sk sc and ch-1 sps, sc in first dc of next dc-group, ch 3, working in front of ch-12 on Part B, dc in next dc, ch 3] around, join with sl st in beg sc. Fasten off.

Outer Border
With size I hook, join baby blue with sc in ch-3 sp between Part B lps on 1 end Motif to left of joining, **[ch 3, sc in next ch sp] 6 times, ch 3, (dc, ch 4, dc in top of last dc, dc) in next ch sp, ch 2, (tr, ch 4, sl st in 4th ch from hook, dc in top of last tr made, tr) in next dc, ch 2, (dc, ch 4, dc in top of last dc, dc) in next ch sp, [ch 3, sc in next ch sp] across to joining, *(dc, ch 3, dc) in joining, [ch 3, sc in next ch sp] across to joining, rep from * across to last Motif***, (dc, ch 3, dc) in joining, ch 3, sc in next ch sp, rep from ** around, ending last rep at ***, join. Fasten off.

Tassel
Cut 4 strands of each color, 12 inches in length. Fold in half, pull fold through ch-4 sp at 1 end of Scarf, pull ends of strands through fold. Pull to tighten. Trim ends.

Rep on other end of Scarf.

HAT
MOTIF
Make 4 Motifs and join them tog forming circle.

Top
Rnd 1: Working around 1 edge of Motifs, with size I hook, join baby blue with dc in any ch sp, dc in same ch sp, evenly sp 70 more dc around, join with sl st in top of beg dc. (72 dc)

Rnd 2: Ch 3 *(counts as first dc)*, dc in each st around, join.

Rnd 3: Ch 3, **dc dec** *(see Stitch Guide)* in next 2 sts, [dc in next st, dc dec in next 2 sts] around, join. (48 dc)

Rnd 4: Ch 3, dc in each st around, join.

Rnd 5: Ch 3, dc dec in next 2 sts, [dc in next st, dc dec in next 2 sts] around, join. (32 dc)

Rnds 6–8: Ch 3, dc in each st around, join.

Rnd 9: [Ch 3, sc in next st] around, join. Fasten off.

Cut 24-inch length of Catskills. Tie a knot in each end. Weave through sts of rnd 7, pull tight and tie ends in a bow. ❑❑

Little Sister Poncho, Headband & Pouch

SKILL LEVEL

INTERMEDIATE

FINISHED SIZES
Headband: Fits 18- to 22-inch head
Poncho: One size fits most
Pouch: 3 x 6 inches

MATERIALS
- Red Heart Kids medium (worsted) weight yarn (5 oz/302 yds/140g per skein):
  4 skeins #2001 white
  2 skeins each #2652 lime and #2734 pink
- Lion Brand Fun Fur bulky (chunky) weight yarn (1.75 oz /64 yds/50g per skein):
  4 skeins #194 lime
- Size G/6/4mm crochet hook or size needed to obtain gauge
- Tapestry needle

GAUGE
Each Motif is 4 inches square

SPECIAL STITCHES
Picot: Ch 3, sl st in top of last st made.

Joining chain space (j-ch sp): Ch 2, sc in corresponding ch sp on last Motif, ch 1.

INSTRUCTIONS
PONCHO
FIRST MOTIF
Part A
With pink, ch 4, sl st in first ch to form ring, ch 1, [sc in ring, ch 12] 8 times, join with sl st in beg sc. Fasten off. *(8 sc, 8 ch sps)*

Part B
Rnd 1: With lime Kids yarn, ch 7, tr in 7th ch from hook *(next 6 chs count as first tr and ch-2)*, [ch 2, tr in same ch] 6 times, join with sl st in 4th ch of beg ch-6. *(8 tr, 8 ch sps)*
Rnd 2: Sl st to ch sp, ch 3 *(counts as first dc)*, (dc, **picot**—see Special Stitches, 2 dc) in same ch sp, *(2 dc, ch 8, 2 dc) in next ch sp**, (2 dc, picot, 2 dc) in next ch sp, rep from * around, ending last rep at **, join with sl st in top of beg ch-3. Fasten off.

Place Part A behind Part B, matching centers, pull Part A ch-12 sps through ch-2 sps on Part B, then pull ch-8 sps on Part B through every other ch-12 sp of Part A for corners.

Border
Join white with sc in ch-12 sp of Part A and picot of Part B at same time, ch 3, sc in same place, *ch 3, sc between dc groups on Part B, ch 3, (3 dc, ch 3, 3 dc) in corner ch sp, ch 3, sc between dc groups on Part B, ch 3**, (sc, ch 3, sc) in next ch-12 sp and next picot at same time, rep from * around, ending last rep at **, join. Fasten off.

JOINED MOTIF
Make 35.
Part A
Work same as Part A of First Motif.

Part B
Work same as Part B of First Motif.

Border
Join white with sc in ch-12 sp of Part A and picot of Part B at same time, ch 3, sc between dc groups on Part B, ch 3, (3 dc, **j-ch sp**—see Special Stitches, 3 dc) in corner ch sp, j-ch sp, sc between dc groups on Part B,

12 CELTIC CROCHET ACCESSORIES • Annie's Attic • Berne, IN 46711 • www.AnniesAttic.com

ch 3, (sc, j-ch sp, sc) in next ch-12 sp and next picot at same time, ch 3, sc between dc groups on Part B, j-ch sp, (3 dc, j-ch sp, 3 dc) in next corner ch sp, *ch 3, sc between dc groups on Part B, ch 3**, (sc, picot, sc) in next ch-12 sp and picot at same time, ch 3, sc between dc groups on Part B, ch 3, (3 dc, ch 3, 3 dc) in corner ch sp, rep from * around, ending last rep at **, join. Fasten off.

Work Joined Motif, joining across as many sides as needed to join Motifs according to illustration. Join last row of Motif matching X's.

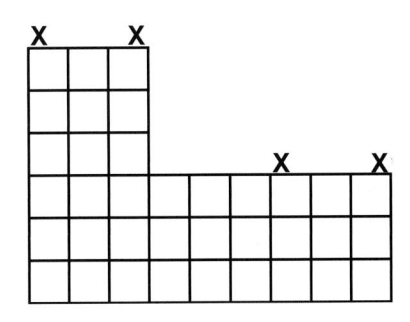

Neck Ribbing
Row 1: With white, ch 21, sc in 2nd ch from hook and in each ch across, turn. *(20 sc)*
Rows 2–38: Working in **back lps** *(see Stitch Guide),* ch 1, sc in each st across, turn. At end of last row, fasten off.

Sew short ends tog forming a tube.
Next row: Holding 2 strands of fun fur tog as 1, working in ends of rows around 1 edge of tube, join with sc in end of first row, sc in each row around, join with sl st in beg sc. Fasten off.
Next row: Rep last rnd on opposite end of tube.

Sew on Neck Ribbing to neck edge of Poncho with WS tog.

HEADBAND
Make and join 4 Motifs in a circle
Working around top edge of Motifs, holding 2 strands of Fun Fur tog as 1, evenly sp sc around, join with sl st in beg sc. Fasten off.
Rep around bottom edge.

POUCH
Rnd 1: With 2 strands Fun Fur, ch 18, sl st in first ch to form ring, ch 1, sc in each ch around, join with sl st in beg sc.
Rnds 2–16: Ch 1, sc in each st around, join. At end of last rnd, fasten off.
Flatten and sew one end closed.

Cord
With white, ch 2, sc in 2nd ch from hook, **turn** to left, sc in vertical side of bars of sc *(see illustration 1)*, [**turn** to left again and sc in side bars of sc *(see illustration 2)*] until Cord measure 36 inches or desired length. Fasten off.

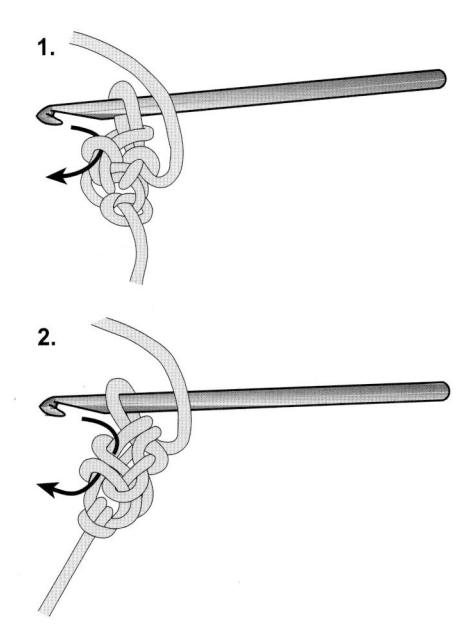

Sew ends of Cord to inside top edge of Pouch for handle.

Big Sister Poncho & Scarf

SKILL LEVEL
INTERMEDIATE

FINISHED SIZES
Scarf: 3½ x 64 inches
Poncho: One size fits most

MATERIALS
- Red Heart Kids medium (worsted) weight yarn (5 oz/302 yds/140g per skein):
  6 skeins #2734 pink
  3 skeins each #2252 orange and #2230 yellow
- Bernat Boa medium (worsted) weight yarn (1.75 oz/71 yds/50g per skein):
  3 skeins #81605 tweety bird
- Sizes G/6/4mm and I/9/5.5mm crochet hooks or size needed to obtain gauge
- Tapestry needle

GAUGE
Size G hook: Each Motif is 4 inches square

SPECIAL STITCHES
Picot: ch 3, sl st in top of last st made.

Joining chain space (j-ch sp): Ch 2, sc in corresponding ch sp on last Motif, ch 1.

INSTRUCTIONS
PONCHO
FIRST MOTIF
Part A
With size G hook and yellow, ch 4, sl st in first ch to form ring, ch 1, [sc in ring, ch 12] 8 times, join with sl st in beg sc. Fasten off. *(8 sc, 8 ch sps)*

Part B
Rnd 1: With size G hook and orange, ch 7, tr in 7th ch from hook *(next 4 chs count as first tr and ch-2)*, [ch 2, tr in same ch] 6 times, join with sl st in 5th ch of beg ch-7. *(8 tr, 8 ch sps)*
Rnd 2: Sl st to ch sp, ch 3 *(counts as first dc)*, (dc, **picot**—*see Special Stitches*, 2 dc) in same ch sp, *(2 dc, ch 8, 2 dc) in next ch sp**, (2 dc, picot, 2 dc) in next ch sp, rep from * around, ending last rep at **, join with sl st in top of beg ch-3. Fasten off.
Place Part A behind Part B, matching centers, pull Part A ch-12 sps through ch-2 sps on Part B, then pull ch-8 sps on Part B through every other ch-12 sp of Part A for corners.

Border
With size G hook, join pink with sc in ch-12 sp of Part A and picot of Part B at same time, ch 3, sc in same place, *ch 3, sc between dc groups on Part B, ch 3, (3 dc, ch 3, 3 dc) in corner ch sp, ch 3, sc between dc groups on Part B, ch 3**, (sc, ch 3, sc) in next ch-12 sp and next picot at same time, rep from * around, ending last rep at **, join. Fasten off.

JOINED MOTIF
Make 55.
Part A
Make 28 orange.
Make 27 yellow.
Work same as Part A of First Motif.

14 CELTIC CROCHET ACCESSORIES • Annie's Attic • Berne, IN 46711 • www.AnniesAttic.com

Part B
Make 27 orange.
Make 28 yellow.
Work same as Part B of First Motif.

Border
With size G hook, join pink with sc in ch-12 sp of Part A and picot of Part B at same time, ch 3, sc between dc groups on Part B, ch 3, (3 dc, **j-ch sp**—see Special Stitches, 3 dc) in corner ch sp, j-ch sp, sc between dc groups on Part B, ch 3, (sc, j-ch sp, sc) in next ch-12 sp and next picot at same time, ch 3, sc between dc groups on Part B, j-ch sp, (3 dc, j-ch sp, 3 dc) in next corner ch sp, *ch 3, sc between dc groups on Part B, ch 3**, (sc, picot, sc) in next ch-12 sp and picot at same time, ch 3, sc between dc groups on Part B, ch 3, (3 dc, ch 3, 3 dc) in corner ch sp, rep from * around, ending last rep at **, join. Fasten off.

Work Joined Motif, joining across as many sides as needed to join Motifs according to illustration, join last row of Motifs matching X's.

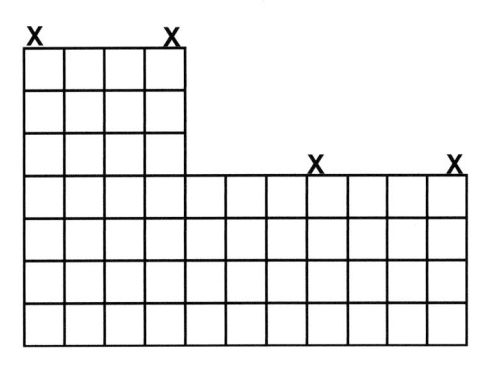

NECK TRIM
Rnd 1: With size G hook, join pink with sc in any ch sp, evenly sp sc around, join with sl st in beg sc.

Rnd 2: Ch 1, sc in each st around, join. Fasten off.

SCARF
Row 1: With size I hook and tweety bird, ch 9, pull up lp in 2nd ch from hook and in each ch across, to work lps off hook, yo, pull through 1 lp on hook, [yo, pull through 2 lps on hook] across, leaving last lp on hook (last lp counts as first lp of next row).

Row 2: Pull up lp in each vertical bar (see illustration) across, to work lps off hook, yo, pull through 1 lp on hook, [yo, pull through 2 lps on hook] across.

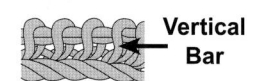

Next rows: Rep row 2 until piece measures 64 inches or length desired. At end of last row, fasten off.

Annie's Attic

306 East Parr Road
Berne, IN 46711
© 2005 Annie's Attic

TOLL-FREE ORDER LINE or to request a free catalog (800) LV-ANNIE (800) 582-6643
Customer Service (800) AT-ANNIE (800) 282-6643, **Fax** (800) 882-6643
Visit www.AnniesAttic.com

We have made every effort to ensure the accuracy and completeness of these instructions. We cannot, however, be responsible for human error, typographical mistakes or variations in individual work. Reprinting or duplicating the information, photographs or graphics in this publication by any means, including copy machine, computer scanning, digital photography, e-mail, personal Web site and fax, is illegal. Failure to abide by federal copyright laws may result in litigation and fines.

ISBN: 1-59635-030-X   All rights reserved   Printed in USA   1 2 3 4 5 6 7 8 9

Stitch Guide

ABBREVIATIONS

beg	begin/beginning
bpdc	back post double crochet
bpsc	back post single crochet
bptr	back post treble crochet
CC	contrasting color
ch	chain stitch
ch-	refers to chain or space previously made (i.e. ch-1 space)
ch sp	chain space
cl	cluster
cm	centimeter(s)
dc	double crochet
dec	decrease/decreases/decreasing
dtr	double treble crochet
fpdc	front post double crochet
fpsc	front post single crochet
fptr	front post treble crochet
g	gram(s)
hdc	half double crochet
inc	increase/increases/increasing
lp(s)	loop(s)
MC	main color
mm	millimeter(s)
oz	ounce(s)
pc	popcorn
rem	remain/remaining
rep	repeat(s)
rnd(s)	round(s)
RS	right side
sc	single crochet
sk	skip(ped)
sl st	slip stitch
sp(s)	space(s)
st(s)	stitch(es)
tog	together
tr	treble crochet
trtr	triple treble
WS	wrong side
yd(s)	yard(s)
yo	yarn over

Chain—ch: Yo, pull through lp on hook.

Slip stitch—sl st: Insert hook in st, yo, pull through both lps on hook.

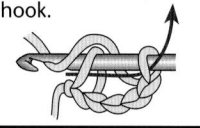

Single crochet—sc: Insert hook in st, yo, pull through st, yo, pull through both lps on hook.

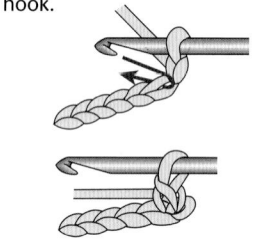

Front loop—front lp / Back loop—back lp

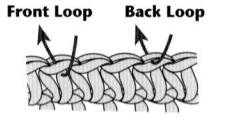

Front post stitch—fp: Back post stitch—bp: When working post st, insert hook from right to left around post st on previous row.

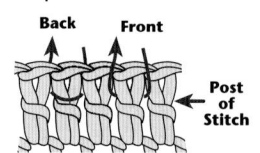

Half double crochet—hdc: Yo, insert hook in st, yo, pull through st, yo, pull through all 3 lps on hook.

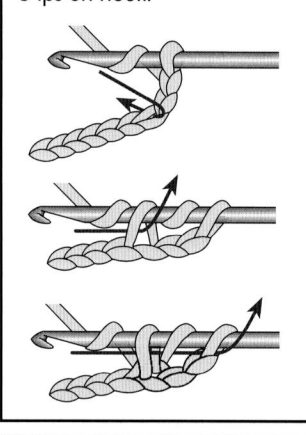

Double crochet—dc: Yo, insert hook in st, yo, pull through st, [yo, pull through 2 lps] twice.

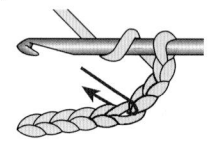

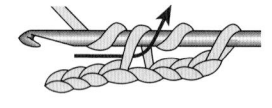

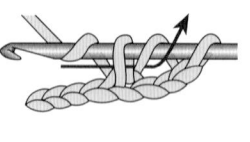

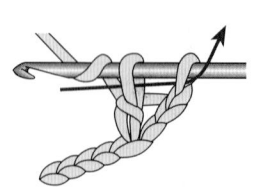

Change colors: Drop first color; with second color, pull through last 2 lps of st.

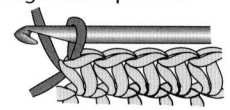

Treble crochet—tr: Yo twice, insert hook in st, yo, pull through st, [yo, pull through 2 lps] 3 times.

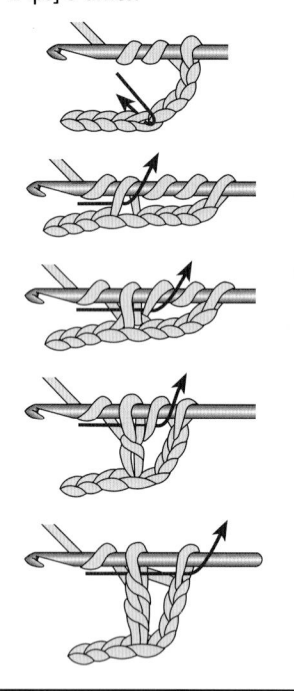

Double treble crochet—dtr: Yo 3 times, insert hook in st, yo, pull through st, [yo, pull through 2 lps] 4 times.

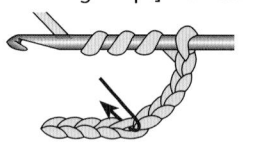

Single crochet decrease (sc dec): (Insert hook, yo, draw up a lp) in each of the sts indicated, yo, draw through all lps on hook.

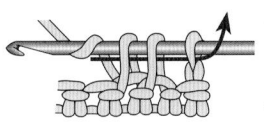

Example of 2-sc dec

Half double crochet decrease (hdc dec): (Yo, insert hook, yo, draw lp through) in each of the sts indicated, yo, draw through all lps on hook.

Example of 2-hdc dec

Double crochet decrease (dc dec): (Yo, insert hook, yo, draw lp through, yo, draw through 2 lps on hook) in each of the sts indicated, yo, draw through all lps on hook.

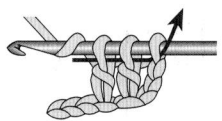

Example of 2-dc dec

US		UK
sl st (slip stitch)	=	sc (single crochet)
sc (single crochet)	=	dc (double crochet)
hdc (half double crochet)	=	htr (half treble crochet)
dc (double crochet)	=	tr (treble crochet)
tr (treble crochet)	=	dtr (double treble crochet)
dtr (double treble crochet)	=	ttr (triple treble crochet)
skip	=	miss

For more complete information, visit

StitchGuide.com